A trip to New Zealand

Laurence Harger

Cornelsen

Cornelsen English Library
Laurence Harger

Verlagsredaktion
Julie Colthorpe

Umschlaggestaltung
Heike Börner, dia
Katrin Nehm

Titelbilder
Rob Cousins, Bristol (li, oben)
mauritius images/Photo New Zealand, Hamburg

Illustration
Constanze Schargan, Berlin
Dr. Volkhard Binder, Berlin (Karte)

Typografie
Anna Bakalović und Annika Preyhs, Berlin

Gestaltung & technische Umsetzung
Ilona und Ingo Ostermaier

www.cornelsen.de
www.EnglishG.de

1. Auflage, 6. Druck 2010

Alle Drucke dieser Auflage sind inhaltlich unverändert und können im Unterricht nebeneinander verwendet werden.

Druck: CS-Druck CornelsenStürtz, Berlin

ISBN 978-3-06-031901-5

Inhalt gedruckt auf säurefreiem Papier aus nachhaltiger Forstwirtschaft.

Contents

4	Chapter 1	Singapore to Christchurch
8	Chapter 2	Welcome to Aotearoa
12	Chapter 3	On the road
16	Chapter 4	Where's Jo?
19	Chapter 5	The town on the lake
26	Chapter 6	The hangi
33	Chapter 7	Lord of the Rings
38	Chapter 8	The bungy jump
41	Chapter 9	At home and in town
48	Chapter 10	The argument
52	Chapter 11	The river
60	Chapter 12	The West Coast
67	Chapter 13	End of the trip
70	Vocabulary	
75	Check your understanding	

Chapter 1 Singapore to Christchurch

Dan could hear a noise. What was it? He didn't know. He was so tired but he couldn't sleep. No, it wasn't a noise. It was music. And voices, thousands of voices. Why did they have to shout like that? He just wanted to sleep. Why were all these people in his bedroom? He opened his eyes and saw ... a horrible monster with black teeth.

"Aaah!" Dan shouted. Then he remembered. He wasn't in bed. He was in a seat with a small TV in front of him. The monster was an orc in one of the Lord of the Rings films. The voices and the music came from his headphones. His twin brother Jo was in the seat next to him. They were on a plane between Singapore and Christchurch in New Zealand. They were on the way to see their mum.

Dan looked at his brother.

"You've been asleep," Jo told him.

"How long?"

"Hours. How can you sleep through Lord of the Rings? I've watched two of the films already and I'm watching the third one now. It's so exciting."

"What time is it?" Dan asked.

"What time is it where?"

"What are you talking about, where? Here, of course."

"Well, do you want to know the time in England, or Singapore, or New Zealand?"

This was too much for Dan. He closed his eyes again.

"Let's see," said his brother. Look, it's five past ten in New Zealand. We'll be in Christchurch soon."

Dan opened his eyes again. He could see his mum again soon. That was a nice thought. He took his headphones off.

Suddenly someone turned on the lights in the plane and a woman's voice spoke to them.

"Good morning everyone! I hope you've had a good flight and slept well. We've got about an hour and a half to go now before we land at Christchurch, and in a moment we'll come round with your breakfast."

"Mmm, breakfast!" Jo said. "I'm really hungry."

"But we've only just had dinner," Dan said. "I'm not hungry."

"Dinner was hours ago, Dan. Just after we left Singapore. That was yesterday evening. It's tomorrow now, tomorrow morning. Let's look out the window. Perhaps we can already see New Zealand."

Dan looked out the window – the sun shone into the plane. All he could see was blue sky and blue sea and a few clouds, white in the sun. There were lines across the sea.

"Waves," he thought. "And what's that little red and white thing? Oh, a ship. It's a ship, on the way to – who knows where?"

"Let me look too," his brother said. "Hmmm. Nothing. Oh, well, tell me when you see New Zealand. I want to see the end of the film before we land."

Jo put his headphones on and looked at the TV in front of him again. Dan looked out at the sky and the clouds and the sea and imagined his mum at Christchurch airport.

When breakfast came Dan was hungry too. He ate everything and drank two cups of tea and an orange juice. He felt much better now.

The woman's voice spoke again. "We're only about half an hour from Christchurch now, so we'll collect the headphones soon. Thank you."

"Oh, no!" Jo said. "They can't do that. My film hasn't finished yet. I won't see the end of it."

"Don't worry. I'm sure Mum has got it on DVD, Jo," Dan told his brother. "You can watch it in Queenstown. She is a Lord of the Rings tour guide, you know."

"Yeah," Jo said. "I suppose you're right. Can you see New Zealand yet?"

"Oh, yes. Sorry, I didn't tell you. I forgot. Look at all those mountains!"

Jo looked out the window and all he could see were mountains and more mountains. They were white with snow and they looked like the white teeth of a wild animal.

"Wow!" Jo said. "That's amazing. I've never seen anything like that before. I can't see any towns anywhere."

As the plane flew on, the high mountains started to disappear. Rivers ran down from the mountains through green hills.

The plane started to go down and the boys could see sheep on the hills and small farms and then a few small towns. Then, before they knew it, the plane landed at Christchurch airport.

"Welcome to Christchurch everyone," the woman's voice said. "The time here in New Zealand is eleven twenty-five am."

Dan looked out the window at the other planes from all over the world. He gave a big smile and said quietly, "Hello, New Zealand. Mum, here we come."

Chapter 2 Welcome to Aotearoa

A woman met Dan and Jo at the plane and took them to one of the immigration officers. She gave them a big smile.

"G'day," she said. "How are you?"

"Fine, thanks." The twins both answered at the same time and then laughed.

The officer smiled again. She looked at the twins and then at the two passports. "I suppose you always talk together. Now which one of you is Daniel," she asked, "and which one is Jonah?"

"I'm Daniel," Jo answered and looked at his brother. Dan said nothing.

"So you're Jonah then," she said to Dan. "How long are you staying in New Zealand, boys?"

"Four weeks," Dan answered. "We're visiting our mum. She lives in Queenstown."

"Queenstown! Oh, it's beautiful there. You'll love it. OK," she said and gave them back their passports. "Now you have a great time in New Zealand. Bye."

They followed the woman again and waited for their bags. When their bags came they went through customs.

"OK, mate," the customs officer said to Jo, "have you got any food with you?"

"Food? Have we got any food, Dan?"

"Yes," Dan said. "Chocolates. Chocolates for our mum."

"Right. Just chocolates?"

"Yes." Dan nodded.

"And what about walking shoes?" the officer asked.

"Walking shoes, yes," Dan said. "Our dad bought them for us. He said we have to have good walking shoes in New Zealand."

"Yes, he's right about that," the officer said. "Let's have a look at them, eh?"

Dan and Jo opened their bags and took out their walking shoes. Dan looked at Jo's shoes. They were still dirty from when they tried them on the Bristol Downs one day.

"Clean your shoes before you come, Mum said. Remember, Jo?" Dan said to his brother and held his clean shoes up.

"No worries, mate," the customs officer said and took Jo's shoes. "We'll clean these for you. You pick them up at the little window on the right when you go out. OK?"

As Dan and Jo walked out, Jo had a big smile on his face. He turned to his brother: "Why clean your own shoes if they do it for you in New Zealand?"

Dan looked up and closed his eyes for a second, but then he had to laugh too. They walked on and pushed open a door. There were people everywhere.

"I can't see Mum anywhere," Dan said.

"She'll be here," Jo said. "Don't worry."

Then they heard her voice. "Dan! Jo!"

Dan dropped his bag and ran to her. His mother gave him a big hug, then held him by the shoulders and said, "Let me have a good look at you."

She smiled at him and said, "Hello, love. I'm so happy you're here."

"Me too, Mum."

Then Jo came over with both their bags.

"Come here, Jo," his mother said and took them both in her arms. They stood there like that for a couple of minutes.

Mrs Thompson had tears in her eyes. So did Dan. "Come on, then. Let's get to the car. We've still got a long way to go today."

"There's our car, over there. The white one," said the twins' mum in the car park. At the same time, a man got out of the car. He had dark hair and a black T-shirt. When he smiled his teeth looked extra white next to his brown skin. He waved to Mrs Thompson and her kids.

"There's Pita," Mrs Thompson said.

When they got to the car, Pita shook both the boys' hands. "Hi, guys. Welcome to Aotearoa, New Zealand."

"Welcome to what?" Jo asked.

"Aotearoa. That's what we call New Zealand in Maori."

"Oh, yeah," Jo said, "that's right. It means Land of the … something or other."

"Land of the long white cloud," Pita told him. "And you'll see lots of those while you're here, guys. Come on. Let's get your bags in the car and get on the road."

"Yeah," Jo said, "Queenstown here we come! Hey, can I sit in the front, Mum? You get a better view in the front."

"Well, OK. I suppose you can," the twins' mother said. "Can you drive first, Pita?"

"Sure. No worries."

"Oh, good," said Dan, "so we can sit in the back and talk, Mum. Right?

"Right."

Chapter 3 On the road

Half an hour after they left Christchurch airport, Jo was asleep in the front seat next to Pita.

"Aren't you tired too, love?" Mrs Thompson asked Dan.

"No, I slept on the plane, Mum. Jo watched films all night."

"That sounds like Jo," his mum said with a smile.

"How long is the journey to Queenstown, Mum?"

"Well, it's about 6 hours and then we'll have to stop a couple of times for a break. I don't think we'll be home before about 8 o'clock this evening. What do you think, Pita?"

"Yeah, that sounds about right," Pita said. He smiled at Dan in the mirror. "Do you think you'll stay awake all that time, Dan?"

Dan looked back at Pita in the mirror for a second, then looked away. "I think so. I'm not tired now and we've ... we've got lots to talk about, right Mum?"

"Yes, we have," said his mother and put her arm round his shoulders. "So, how's your dad?"

For the next hour Dan told his mum all the news from back home in Bristol: about the drive from Bristol to the airport in London; about how nervous their dad was; about his friends at school and their holiday plans; about his school report. His mother told him about her plans for their trip.

All the time, Jo slept like a baby in the front seat. Dan touched his brother on the shoulder, but Jo didn't move or open his eyes. "And he wanted to have the best view!" They all laughed.

At about 2.30 pm, in the small town of Geraldine, Pita stopped the car in front of a café.

"I don't know about you two," he said, "but I need a cup of coffee and something to eat. Shall I wake Jo?"

"No, let him sleep," Mrs Thompson answered.

They got out of the car and went into the café.

"Hello," said the girl in the café when she saw them. "What can I get you?"

"Well, I'll have a flat white," Pita said. "What about you, Cathy?"

When Pita said his mum's name, it sounded like Kethy, Dan thought. They sound funny, these Kiwis.

"A long black for me, please," Dan's mum said. "What about you, Dan?"

"Well, what are you having, Mum? A long black? What's that?"

"Oh, it's just a black coffee. And Pita's having a flat white – that's a coffee with milk but not like a ..."

"OK, Mum, that's enough information about coffee," Dan said. "I don't even like coffee. I'll have a flat brown."

"A what?"

"A flat brown. Isn't that what they call a cup of tea with milk in New Zealand?"

Pita and his mum both laughed. Then Mrs Thompson ordered some sandwiches and they went and sat in the garden. There were only a few people there. It was full of strange trees.

"I've never seen trees like that before," said Dan. "What are they?"

"Well, those on the right are just tree ferns," his mum said. "Like ferns we have back in the UK, but bigger. And then those funny ones over there are cabbage trees – but you can't eat them."

"And those ones there?"

"I don't know their names. Pita? What are they called?"

"Don't know. Palms?"

"Oh, Pita!" Mrs Thompson laughed. "You're Maori but you don't know your New Zealand trees?"

"I don't think they're New Zealand trees," Pita told her. "I think you Pakeha brought them with you."

"What did he call you, Mum? Paki …" Dan asked.

"Pakeha, love," his mum said. "It's the Maori name for white people in New Zealand. White people use it too. So there are Maori, Pakeha and Pasifika people in New Zealand – and they're all Kiwis."

"Lots of Asians now too," Pita said. "New Zealanders come from all over the world."

Twenty minutes later they went back out to the street.

"I suppose your brother is still asleep," Mrs Thompson said to Dan as they looked inside the car. But he wasn't. The car was empty. Jo was gone.

Chapter 4 Where's Jo?

"He's gone," Dan said.

"Yes, I can see that," Dan's mother said. She sounded a little angry.

"Well, he can't be far away," Pita said. "Let's look for him, eh?"

They looked up and down the street but couldn't see Jo anywhere.

"OK," said Pita, "I'll go this way, you two go that way. Then we meet back at the car in ten minutes. OK?"

Dan and his mother walked along the road and looked in all the shops as they went. Pita walked the other way towards a big park. He soon saw Jo in a flower garden and walked up behind him.

"What, you're a flower lover, eh?" he asked.

Jo turned round. "Oh, hello, Pita. Flowers? No way. I saw some kids, they had a ball and they ran into this park with it. But then I lost them."

"I think your mum and your brother are a bit worried about you," Pita said. "Let's go back to the car, eh?"

"OK," Jo agreed, and they started to walk back to the car. "When I woke up you were all gone, so I looked for you. Where were you?"

"In the café next to the car. Didn't you look in there?"

"Café? No, I didn't see a café. But I'm quite hungry now."

"Well, we can get you a takeaway. We have to get back on the road if we want to get to Queenstown tonight."

When they got back to the car, Dan and Mrs Thompson were already there.

"Where have you been?" Mrs Thompson asked Jo. "You can't just go off alone like that. We were worried!"

"Sorry, Mum. But I didn't know you were in the café. So I looked for you that way." He pointed towards the park.

"All right, Jo," his mum said and gave him a hug.

"Jo's hungry," Pita said. "Right, Jo?"

"Yes," said Jo. "Can I get a takeaway and eat it in the car?"

"OK. Come on, let's be quick about it," his mum said and they went back into the café.

Mrs Thompson and Dan sat in the front of the car now. The road took them closer and closer to the mountains and the sun began to drop in the sky and the day grew colder. Their mother turned the heater on and chatted quietly with Pita. The twins were quiet now, tired from their long journey. Soon, as it got darker, they were both asleep.

In his dreams Dan lay in a big, comfortable bed. Someone next to the bed talked quietly to him. It was his mother – he knew her voice. He opened his eyes and his mum and dad smiled at him. He closed his eyes again. It was warm and dark in bed and he felt happy and safe.

When they arrived in Queenstown a few hours later, the twins were still asleep. They opened their eyes when the car stopped in front of Pita and Mrs Thompson's house.

"Welcome to Queenstown, boys," their mum said. "Come on, let's get your bags inside, then you two can go to bed."

As they unpacked the car, it suddenly began to rain. The boys heard the rain before they felt it on their heads and faces. It moved across the lake with a cold wind. It whispered like a strange animal. The whispers grew louder and louder before the rain touched them. This was so different to the rain of Bristol. They realized they really were on the other side of the world.

Chapter 5 The town on the lake

The rain was so heavy it was almost noisier inside the house than out. Half an hour later, after some food and a cup of hot chocolate, the twins were in bed. Mrs Thompson kissed them good night, went out and closed the door.

Dan and Jo listened to the rain. They could hear it on the roof and they were soon asleep.

It rained all night long till morning. Dan and Jo woke early. Dan turned on the lamp next to his bed.

"It's still raining," Jo said. "I'm sure there'll be a flood. They have lots of floods here."

"Yeah," said Dan. "Maybe we'll have to stay at home for days with Mum and they'll come and get us in a boat."

"Yeah, and we'll be on TV and Dad will see us back in Bristol."

"Right," Dan said. "And we'll wave to him and the newspapers will want to interview us when we get home."

" Let's open the curtains and see," Jo said and jumped out of bed. "Boy, it's cold in here."

"Mum said something about a heater last night," Dan said, "but I can't remember what."

He looked round the room while Jo opened the curtains.

"Look, there's a heater. On the floor in the corner there, by that cupboard."

Jo went to the heater and turned it on and then got back into bed.

"Brrrr! It's freezing."

The boys looked out the window but couldn't see very much. A few street lamps and some other houses. Everything else was black. They lay there and listened to the rain.

"What's the time?" Dan asked.

Jo looked at his watch. "Seven. When do you think Mum and Pita get up?"

Then, as suddenly as it came the night before, the rain stopped and the house was very quiet. Outside the sky was getting grey and they could see more.

"Look at all that water," Jo said. "There is a flood."

Dan laughed and threw a pillow at his brother. "Don't be stupid. That's the lake."

Dan and Jo looked out across Lake Wakatipu and then, slowly, at about 7.30, the sun came up over the mountains on the other side. They could see lots of snow at the top.

"Wow," said Dan. "The lake is really huge. And the mountains."

"Yes, what's the highest mountain again?" Jo asked.

"Mount Cook," Dan answered just as someone knocked on the door.

"Come in," Jo said.

The door opened and Pita came in.

"Aoraki, we call it," he said.

"What?" said Jo.

"Aoraki," Pita repeated. "That's Mount Cook's real name."

"In Maori?" Dan asked.

"That's it. Aoraki. It means cloud piercer because it's so high it goes up through the clouds. So, how are you two doing? Did you get enough sleep?"

"Yes, but we've been awake for a long time," Dan answered. "Is Mum up?"

"She is. Are you guys ready for breakfast?"

"Yeah. Brekkie!" Jo shouted. "I'm really hungry."

The twins got dressed quickly and went into the kitchen. It was the warmest room in the house.

"We live in the kitchen in winter," the twins' mum said. "In the winter this house is so cold and this is the only room we can keep warm all the time. I really miss my central heating."

"You Poms," said Pita, "you're always cold. Just put more clothes on. That's what we Kiwis say. No worries."

Mrs Thompson laughed and hit Pita on the arm with a towel. Then they all sat down at the table and had breakfast. There was tea and orange juice and cornflakes and toast.

"Just like our breakfast in Bristol," said Jo as he took his second piece of toast. "Can I have another cup of tea, Mum?"

"Yes, of course you can. Pass me your cup," Mrs Thompson said.

"What's the plan today, Mum?" Dan asked.

"Well, I don't have to go to work today or tomorrow, so we can do what we want."

"Let's go bungy jumping!" Jo said.

"No, let's just stay here and talk, Mum," Dan said.

"What's the weather forecast, Pita?" Mrs Thompson asked.

"Well, it's good for this morning," Pita answered, "but rain maybe later this afternoon."

"All right," Mrs Thompson said. "Well, why don't we go into town this morning and ..."

"... and go bungy jumping," Jo said.

"... and have a look round," his mother went on. "The bungy jumping place isn't in town. We have to drive there."

"Well, can we go tomorrow, then?" Jo asked.

"I think so. If the weather is OK. So, we'll go into town now and then we can come back in the afternoon and have a chat. OK, Dan?"

"OK," Dan said.

Pita and Mrs Thompson's house was in a road on the side of a hill. Dan and Jo and their mum left the house and walked along the road and then went down the hill on the left. Soon they were at the edge of the lake. The snow on the mountains on the other side was very white in the morning sun. Jo ran down between some trees to the water and put his hand in.

"Brrrr! It's freezing! We can't go swimming in that," he shouted.

"Well, not in winter, you can't," Mrs Thompson said. "Some people go swimming in the summer. Not me. It's always too cold for me."

They walked along the beach by the side of the road and past some boat houses. Then they walked across a park and a few minutes later they were back next to the lake with the centre of town on their right. It was much busier there with lots of cars and shops and cafés and people everywhere.

For the next few hours they walked around the streets of Queenstown and along the lake. The town was full of tourists.

"Tourists are important here," Mrs Thompson told Dan and Jo. "That's how most people make their money."

"You too, Mum," said Dan.

"That's right, Dan. And I love my job."

"I can't wait for the Lord of the Rings tour, Mum," said Jo. "When can we go?"

"Oh, Thursday, I think," his mum answered.

They had a drink in a café and when they came out the sun was gone and the clouds looked grey and full of rain.

"OK," said Mrs Thompson. "Let's walk back home the quick way."

By the time they got home, the rain was already quite heavy.

Chapter 6 The hangi

The next day was very sunny again and when the twins came into the kitchen for breakfast Mrs Thompson said, "Pita has got a surprise for you."

"Yeah," Pita began. "A couple of my mates do great hangis."

"Great what?" asked Dan.

"Hangis. A hangi is a traditional Maori meal. So I spoke to Turoa and Billy this morning, my two mates, and as the weather is so good they said, 'Why don't we do a hangi? Cathy's kids can help.' Well, what do you think?"

"Yeah, great," said Jo. "What do we have to do?"

"I don't know. Turoa and Billy will tell you. We'll go over there after breakfast."

After breakfast they all got in the car and drove across Queenstown to Turoa's house. Turoa and Billy were in the garden. Turoa was older than Pita and Billy was a bit younger. They came over to the car as it stopped in front of the garage.

"Kia ora koutou," Turoa said. "How are you, Cathy?"

"Hello, Turoa," Mrs Thompson said. "OK,thanks. These are my two boys. Jo ..."

"Kia ora, Jo. Nice to meet you."

"Nice to meet you, Mr ..." Jo said.

"Just call me Turoa. And you must be Dan."

"Yes, hello Turoa."

"And this is Billy," Turoa said.

"Hello, Jo. Dan," Billy said. "Ready for some hard work?"

"Yeah," Jo answered. "What do we have to do?"

"Well, the first two jobs are: one – dig a big hole. And two – make a fire. What do you want to do?"

"Make the fire," Jo and Dan said together.

"I see," said Turoa. "So we old guys have to dig the hole, eh? All right. But, before you make the fire, you have to chop the wood. It's in the garage."

There was lots of wood in the garage and two axes.

"I've never chopped wood before," Jo said.

"Come on," Pita said. "I'll show you."

He took a large piece of wood and then he picked up an axe and chopped the wood in half. He chopped the two pieces in half again and then again.

"We need a lot of really small pieces of wood first when we start the fire," Pita said. "Then we can put bigger pieces on. OK, you two try."

It was much harder than it looked, but half an hour later the twins had enough wood. They went back into the garden where Turoa and Billy stood next to a big hole.

"Do we make the fire in the hole?" Dan asked them.

"That's right," Turoa said. "We make the fire in the hole."

"I'll get some paper from the house," Billy said and went inside. He soon came back out with some old newspapers.

Dan and Jo put the paper in the hole and then lots of the small pieces of wood on top of the paper. In a couple of minutes they had a nice little fire and they started to put larger pieces of wood on. After fifteen minutes they had a really good fire.

"Do we cook the food on the fire?" Dan asked.

"Ah wait and see," Turoa answered.

"Where is the food?" Jo asked. "I'm hungry."

Billy laughed. "It'll be a few hours before the food is ready."

"Yes," said Turoa. "Don't you worry about the food. We're not finished here yet. You see those big stones over there in the corner? Bring them over here, please."

The twins carried the big stones over to the fire, one by one.

"Right," said Turoa, "now we can start. Put them into the fire."

They put all the big stones into the fire.

"Now we can go inside and have a sandwich," Billy said. "If you're still hungry."

In the kitchen, Turoa's wife Eileen had lots of food in foil in big metal baskets. She said hello to the twins and gave them both a big kiss.

"Have you ever had a hangi before, boys?" she asked.

"No," Dan answered. "What's in it?"

"Well, it's all in these baskets here. We've got fish and a couple of chooks."

"Chooks?" said Dan

"Chickens," said Eileen. "That's what you call them, I suppose. And we've got lots of different vegetables: carrots and potatoes and kumaras and ..."

"What are kumaras?" Dan asked.

"They're like sweet potatoes, you know?" Eileen said. "Look, I'll show you."

She opened up one of the packets of foil. "Look, we've got the orange kumaras and the white ones. They're delicious. You'll see." Then she turned to her husband. "When will the stones be hot enough, Turoa?" she asked.

"Oh, about an hour and a half."

"OK," his wife said. "Are you hungry, boys? I'll make you a sandwich, eh?"

An hour and a half later everyone was back outside. Turoa held his hands over the stones.

"Yes," he said, "they're hot enough. Come on Billy."

Billy and Turoa quickly took the wood out of the hole. Then Billy put a large, wet sack on the stones. There was a loud noise and a lot of steam. Then Pita and Turoa put the baskets of food on top of the sack.

Billy threw a second sack on top and then he and Turoa quickly put lots of earth on top of the sack.

"That's it," said Turoa. "Now we wait."

"How long?" asked Dan.

"About three hours," Turoa said. "And then you'll have the best meal of your lives."

A couple of hours later, Dan and Jo were in the garden again when a boy and a girl came along the road. They were both wearing a dark blue school uniform. The boy looked older than the twins, the girl was about the same age. They stopped in front of Turoa's house.

"Hey," the boy said.

"Hi," said Jo and walked over to them. Dan followed him.

"I'm Sam. So, what are you doing in our garden?"

"We're helping with the hangi," Jo said. "Oh, I'm Jo. And this is Dan."

"What?" asked the girl. "Your grandad and Billy are doing a hangi? Why didn't you tell me, Sam?"

"I didn't know, Jessie. That's why. When is the hangi ready?"

Dan looked at his watch. "About half past four, I think."

"Cool. Will you come over then, Jessie?" Sam asked the girl.

"Of course I will. I can't miss a hangi. What's it for?"

"I don't know," said Sam and he looked at Dan and Jo.

"I think it's for us," Dan said. "We're on holiday here. We're visiting our mum."

"Oh, right," said Sam. "You're Cathy's kids. Now I remember. Is Cathy here? And Pita?"

"Yeah, they're inside," Jo said.

"Where are you two from?" Jessie asked.

"From Bristol," Dan said.

"Where's that?"

"In England," Jo said.

"Oh, right. Wow," Jessie said. "How long are you here for?"

"Four weeks."

The four children chatted for another five minutes. Then Jessie said, "OK. I have to go. See you later."

Sam and Dan and Jo went inside.

At 4.30 there were a lot of people in Turoa and Eileen's garden. Turoa and Billy opened up the hole again and picked up the baskets of food. Everyone followed them into the house.

Billy put the baskets down on the dining room table and Eileen started to open up the foil packets.

"Hmmm. That smells fantastic," said Jo.

"Wait till you taste it," said Jessie. "It's the best food in the world. Turoa and Billy do the best hangis in Queenstown."

Everyone went to the table and got their food. Jo and Dan loved it. They finished their first plate and went back to the table. Eileen asked them what they wanted.

"More chook and koo … what's it called?" said Jo.

"Kumara. White or orange?" Eileen asked him.

"Both!" Jo said.

"Same for me," said Dan with a laugh. "Chook and kumara."

A few hours later, Jo and Dan were on the sofa in the living room with Sam and Jessie. Some women on the floor started to sing Maori songs. Dan suddenly felt very tired and closed his eyes.

"You'll be asleep soon," Jessie told him.

He opened his eyes again. "No, I won't," he said. Then he laughed. "Yes, I will. Jet lag. We only got here two days ago."

"Wow," said Jessie. "I've never been on a plane."

"It was really cool," Jo told her. "You get your own TV. I watched all the Lord of the Rings films."

"My dad worked on those films," Jessie said. "He was a driver. He had to drive the actors and other people to the locations. Are you going on one of your mum's tours?"

"Yes, tomorrow, I think," Jo said.

"Why don't you two come too?" Dan suggested.

"No way," said Sam. "Have you ever heard of school?"

"Oh, right," said Dan.

"Anyway, we can do our own tour, right Jess?" Sam said. Then he took the girl's hand and went out into the garden.

At about 8 o'clock, Mrs Thompson drove Dan and Jo home. They were so tired that they went to bed at once.

Chapter 7 Lord of the Rings

Mrs Thompson opened the door to the twins' bedroom and turned on the light as she went inside.

"Come on you two," she said. "Time to get up."

Jo put the pillow over his head. Dan opened one eye.

"It's dark, Mum. Go away, it's still night," he said.

Mrs Thompson pulled the pillow off Jo's head. "Come on. It's seven o'clock. I've phoned the office. You two can go on one of this morning's tours and it leaves at 8.15."

An hour later Mrs Thompson and the twins were in the Lord of the Rings tour office. A big man in shorts came in.

"Hey Cath!" he said and smiled at them all. "So these are your kids."

"Hi Mike. This is Dan. And this is Jo."

"Hi Dan. Hi Jo. Nice to meet you," Mike said and shook both the boys' hands. "I hope you guys are Lord of the Rings fans."

"Yeah, I am," said Jo. "I watched all the films on the plane."

"Is that right?" Mike said and then he took Jo by the shoulders.

"Let me have a look at your eyes," he went on and looked into Jo's eyes. Jo gave Dan and his mum a worried look.

"Ah, yes," Mike said. "It's just as I thought. Your eyes are square from too much TV and video." Then he winked at Jo and laughed.

"OK, see you outside in five minutes," he said and went into another room.

"Square Eyes," Dan said to his brother. Jo just smiled.

"Mike is a real Lord of the Rings fan, Jo," the twins' mum said. "From a long time before the films. He loved the book when he was a kid and he and his friends had Lord of the Rings parties. "

"What book?" Jo asked.

There were two big cars for the tour. Mrs Thompson drove one, Mike the other. As there was only one empty seat in Mrs Thompson's car, Jo went with Mike.

"So you're coming with me, Square Eyes, is that right?" Mike said. "OK, get in, and let's get on the road."

Jo sat next to Mike at the front of the car. There were six other people in the car. An old American couple; they wanted to go on the tour so they could tell their grandchildren in Florida about it. There were also four young students, a man and woman from the UK, an American guy in his twenties and a young German too. The German had clothes on, like Frodo's in the films.

As they drove, Mike told them about the tour. There were locations for the Lord of the Rings films all over New Zealand and this tour went to some of the locations near Queenstown.

The countryside around Queenstown was beautiful, with the mountains full of snow, the sun on the lake, the rivers and the blue sky.

They drove off the main roads and on to small tracks. When they got to a film location, Mike asked who knew it. The students from the UK and the USA were real fans and they guessed right sometimes.

"OK, folks," said Mike and stopped next to a river. "Where are we now?"

"I think I know it," said the English girl as they all got out of the car. "It's where Isildur falls in the river."

"Who falls in the river?" asked Jo.

"Isildur," she answered. "You know, the one who got the ring in the very first film, right at the beginning. I should win something for that."

"Yeah, well done," her friend said. "He rides through here."

"Yeah, right," the American student said. "And the orcs get him. Isildur. Yeah."

"Well done," Mike said. "Isildur and the others came down this track here and the orcs jumped on his back. So he put on the ring and ran into the river. But then the ring fell into the river and the orcs killed Isildur and the ring disappeared for 2000 years. So that was right here, folks. Right here."

"Wow," said Jo, and he looked at the river and the forest and tried to imagine the orcs in the trees and Isildur on his horse. The German student was very quiet. He looked at everything and just smiled.

"He really is in another world," thought Jo.

The tour went on from location to location. The young tourists tried to guess what happened there in the films, even the German student. Mike said "Right!" or "Wrong!" and then explained what happened. "Those are the Misty Mountains in the film", or "That was where the city of Minas Tirith was" or "They filmed one of the big battles here".

At about 10.30, they stopped near the Arrow River for morning tea. They could see the snow on the mountains but in the sun it was quite warm. Mike and Mrs Thompson made the tea and there were biscuits and small cakes. Dan and Jo went down to the river with their tea.

"Did you remember any of the locations from the films?" Jo asked his brother.

"I haven't seen the films. Remember?"

"Oh, right. Mike knows everything about the locations and the films," Jo went on. "He's great."

"Mum knows it all too," Dan said. "And she knows about the book."

"What book?"

"The Lord of the Rings, stupid. It was a book first, you know. It must be fantastic. Better than the films."

"Oh," said Jo. In his head he thought, "How can a book be better than those films?" But he didn't tell Dan that.

When they left again after their tea break, Mike drove along the river slowly, then suddenly turned towards the river and went faster.

"Hold on, folks. Let's see if we can get across the river here."

Jo put his hand over his mouth.

Mike laughed. "No worries, mate."

He drove the car into the river. It went up and down and the water came up to the door. In the middle of the river Mike stopped the car. He put his hand over his mouth and gave Jo a worried look.

"Can you swim?" he asked.

"What's wrong?" Jo said.

Then Mike laughed again and started the car. They drove slowly across to the other side of the river.

"Phew!" said Mike. "We just made it."

On the way back to Queenstown, they passed the famous bungy jump at Kawarau Bridge. They stopped and watched. A young Japanese girl jumped off the bridge and gave a big shout. She fell forty metres towards the river below and then went up and down on the bungy rope.

Jo cheered. "Fantastic! Can we do it tomorrow, Mum?"

"OK," said Mrs Thompson, "if the weather is nice."

Chapter 8 The bungy jump

The next afternoon the twins were back at the bungy jump bridge with Pita. Mrs Thompson was on another Lord of the Rings tour.

"Well," Pita asked Dan. "Do you want to jump?"

"I'm not sure," Dan answered. "It's really high."

"Nah, mate," said Pita. "No worries. It's only forty-something metres. The big jump is over 120. Now that is high."

Dan didn't look very happy about it, but he said, "All right. I'll do it."

They bought their tickets for the jump.

"OK," said one of the guys from the bungy jump place, "let's see how much you weigh."

"What's that for?" asked Dan.

"Well, we have to know how much rope to give you," the guy said. "You don't want to hit the bottom of the river, eh?"

"No way," said Dan.

"Forty-four kilos. Right, now, do you want to stop before the water, or actually touch the water, or go right in?"

"I want to stop before the water, please," Dan answered. "It's freezing."

"Right," the bungy guy said. "Now, who wants to go first?"

Jo wanted to go first, of course. But when he got to the jump platform and looked down, he suddenly realised how high 43 metres is. He turned around and went back.

"What's wrong, mate?" asked Pita.

"It's … it's really high, Pita."

"Well, you know, you don't have to do it if you don't want to. What about you, Dan?" Pita asked.

Dan looked down at the river, then at the platform, and said, "OK."

Out on the platform they tied the bungy rope around his legs.

"Ready?"

"Yes," Dan said quietly.

"OK, move your feet to the edge. Put you arms out. And off you go."

Dan screamed as he jumped off the platform and fell towards the river.

When the bungy rope pulled him back before he touched the water he shouted "I did it, Jo. I did it!"

Jo cheered and shouted as Dan jumped. Then he walked back out to the platform and a few minutes later he screamed too, as he fell towards the river 43 metres below.

Chapter 9 At home and in town

Mrs Thompson had to work for the next few days and the weather wasn't too good. The wind was very strong from the south and it was much colder. When the twins woke up one morning, there was snow in the garden.

"What are your plans for today?" Mrs Thompson asked at breakfast. "You've only got a few more days in Queenstown, remember. We're going off on our trip next week."

"Have you got the Lord of the Rings films on DVD, Mum?" Jo asked. "I want to see the end of the last film."

"No, I haven't, Jo," she answered. "But we've got them at work. I'll bring them home this evening."

"Thanks, Mum."

"Mum?" said Dan.

"Yes, dear."

"Is there a library in town?"

"Of course there is. Why?"

"Can I borrow books?"

"I think so. If I take you, we can get you a library card. Why? What do you want?"

"The Lord of the Rings."

"Oh," said Mrs Thompson. "You don't have to go to the library for that. Go and look in the living room. You'll find it there."

Before she left, Mrs Thompson said to Dan and Jo, "You must write to your dad. And your grandma. You promised. OK?"

When she was gone, Jo said, "If you write to Dad, I'll do Grandma. OK?"

"All right," said Dan. Then he went into the living room and looked at all the books on the shelves. He soon found the Lord of the Rings because it was so thick.

He went back to the kitchen where it was warm and sat down and opened the book and started to read:

Three Rings for the Elven-Kings under the sky,
Seven for the Dwarf-Lords in their halls of stone,
...

Jo was at the computer next to the window.

"What's the time in England, Dan?" he asked.

Dan looked at his watch. "9.30. Yesterday evening. Why?"

"9.30. So Grandma won't be in bed yet. Let's see if she's online."

For the next twenty minutes Dan read his book and Jo sat at the computer. At last Grandma answered.

WelshGranny	Hello, Jo!
madtwin	Hi Gran! not in bed yet?
WelshGranny	No. How r u?
madtwin	gr8. It's snowing here.
WelshGranny	Have u made a snowman?
madtwin	not enough snow.
WelshGranny	What r u doing?
madtwin	mum's at work. dan's reading. i'm chatting with u.
WelshGranny	tell me about ur holiday.
madtwin	fantastic. bungy jumping yesterday. really scary.
WelshGranny	Did Dan do it?

madtwin yes. he went 1st. :-) LOTR tour the day before that.
WelshGranny ur mum's tour?
madtwin yes.
WelshGranny Did u like it?
madtwin yeah.
WelshGranny tell me.

Jo chatted with his grandma, Dan read his book, and the morning passed. At lunchtime, they put some food from yesterday's dinner in the microwave and had lunch.

"Have you written to Dad yet?" Jo asked.

"How?" his brother answered. "You've been on the computer all the time."

"I was chatting with Grandma. She's gone to bed now."

"All right. I'll write Dad an e-mail after lunch. And you?"

"I don't know," said Jo.

"Do you want to read the Lord of the Rings?" Dan asked. "It's really good."

"Er ... maybe. Let me have a look at it."

Dan went and got the book and gave it to Jo. Jo looked at the last page.

"It's over 1000 pages long, Dan," he said.

"So?"

"How can you read a book that long?" Jo said and shook his head. "You're mad."

"Don't be silly, Jo, lots of people read it. It's really exciting. I'm already on page 100."

Jo looked at page 100 and read a bit. Then he looked at Dan.

“They sound … well, old-fashioned. They don’t talk like that in the film,” he said.

He closed the book and gave it back to Dan. “No, I don’t think I’ll read it,” he said. “We can watch the DVD tonight when Mum gets home.”

“I’m going to read the book,” Dan said. “Films are never as good as the books.”

After lunch Jo said, “I think I’ll walk into town and go to Mum’s office. Then I can come home with her.”

Dan looked out the window. “The snow has stopped. But it’s raining now,” he said.

“Not much,” Jo said and went to get his coat.

After Jo left, Dan went to the computer and wrote an e-mail to their dad and told him all about their trip so far.

Jo was on his way to their mum’s office when he met Sam and Jessie in front of a shoe shop.

“Hey, Jo!” Jessie said and gave him a big smile.

“Oh, hi Jessie. Sam. What are you doing here?”

“We’re just hanging out after school,” Sam answered. “How about you?”

“I’m going to my Mum’s office.”

“Oh, yeah?” said Sam. “Is she on another tour?”

“Yes,” Jo said.

“Where’s your brother?” Jessie asked.

“He’s at home,” Jo told them. “He’s reading. Lord of the Rings. Too long for me.”

“Yeah, I like the films better,” Sam said. “So, what are you doing on Saturday?”

“I don’t know. We’re going away next week to the West Coast.”

"We could go on a Lord of the Rings tour together," Sam said.

"Well," Jo said, "I could ask my mum, but ..."

"No, not with your mum," Sam said. "We can go on our own tour. I'll take my grandad's car."

"Don't be silly!" Jo said. "You're too young ..."

"I'm almost 16," Sam said. "I've got my driver's licence. Look. Here it is."

Sam showed Jo his driver's licence. Jo couldn't believe it. "You have to be 17 to get a licence in Britain."

"15 here," Sam said. "Right, Jessie?"

"Yeah," Jessie said, "but ..."

"No buts," Sam went on. "I'll get my grandad's car and we'll do our own tour. I know the best locations."

They talked about the idea for a few minutes. Then Sam said, "So we'll meet you here at ten on Saturday. Bring your brother – er ... but don't tell anyone, right? See you."

Jo went to his mum's office and waited for her there. At about 4.30 Mrs Thompson came back from her tour and then they went home together. Dan was asleep in his chair at the table, with his book in front of him.

"Ssshhh!" said Mrs Thompson to Jo when they opened the kitchen door and saw Dan. Too late. Dan opened his eyes.

Jo held up the DVD of Lord of the Rings. "You can forget your book, now," he said. "This is the real thing."

Dan looked at his mum and shook his head. Suddenly there was a strange noise and the house began to shake. Dan thought, "Why is the whole house shaking when I shake my head?"

Mrs Thompson grabbed Jo and pushed him over to the table.

"Under the table," she shouted. "Quick. Quick! It's an earthquake."

Chapter 10 The argument

The earthquake was only a few seconds long. They all waited under the table for a few minutes. Then Mrs Thompson said, "OK. I think that was it."

They all got out from under the table and Mrs Thompson turned on the radio.

"Yes, that was an earthquake in the Queenstown area just now folks. You didn't imagine it. When we have more news about it, you'll hear it first here on More FM."

Mrs Thompson turned the radio off again.

"Wow!" said Jo. "An earthquake. Wait till we tell the kids at school about it!"

"Have you ever felt one before, Mum?" asked Dan.

"Oh, yes, love. We have quite a lot of earthquakes in New Zealand," Mrs Thompson answered. "You can't even feel most of them because they are so small. But when you do feel one, you have to be careful. It could be a big one."

"What," said Jo, "you mean the house could fall down or something like that?"

"Something like that, yes."

"Cool!" said Jo.

"Not if you're in the house, Jo. Earthquakes aren't a joke."

The next few days the weather was warmer again and the snow disappeared. The twins' mother had to work all that week before she started her holiday the next week. Pita had some free time so he took the boys on some short trips.

Before they left one morning, the three of them had breakfast in the kitchen. Pita said, "We can go for a nice walk to a waterfall today. Have you got walking shoes?"

"Yeah," said Dan. "We've got new ones."

The twins went up to their room. Pita followed them up the stairs.

"Look," said Dan. "Here they are."

"Oh, they look good. Jo?"

"Hmmm. I can't find them," said Jo.

"They cleaned them for you at the airport, Jo, remember?" Dan said.

"At the airport? Oh, no!"

"What?" said Pita. "Oh, Jo, don't say that you left them at the airport!"

"Yes, I think I did."

Pita went downstairs and phoned Christchurch Airport. He was on the phone for about ten minutes. When he came back upstairs he said, "Yes, they've got your shoes, Jo. And they're going to send them, so you'll have them for your trip next week. What size are you? We can probably find an old pair for you at the office for today."

The boys liked their trips with Pita, but on Saturday, Pita had to work too.

"What can we do today, Mum?" Dan asked before Mrs Thompson left for her morning tour.

"Oh, I don't know, love. You could take a walk over to Turoa's."

"That's a good idea," Dan said. "What do you think, Jo?"

"Oh, maybe. We can decide later."

"All right, boys. Call me and let me know where you are. Bye."

Half an hour later Dan said, "Are you ready, Jo? Let's go to Turoa's."

"Oh, why don't we just walk into town?" Jo asked.

"What do you want to do in town?" Dan asked.

"Oh, you know, just look around. Maybe we'll meet somebody."

"Meet somebody?" Dan said. "Jo, we don't know anybody here."

"We know a few people. Come on, it'll be more fun in town."

Twenty minutes later they walked through the park and into the centre of Queenstown. The streets and shops were busy. Jo stopped in front of a shoe shop.

"Come on, Jo," his brother said. "Your walking shoes will be here soon. You don't have to buy new ones."

"I'm just looking," Jo said, and he looked in the window and then up and down the street.

"Just looking?" Dan said. "But what are you looking for?"

A big car stopped in the road in front of the shop. The window opened and Jessie looked out.

"Hi, Jo. Dan. Get in."

Jo got into the back of the car. "Come on, Dan."

Dan followed his brother into the back of the car and sat down. "Where are we going?" he asked.

Sam turned round and looked at the twins. "On our own Lord of the Rings Tour."

"What?" Dan said. He looked at his brother. "You planned this, right?"

"Well, yes," Jo answered, "but I didn't tell you … well because I knew …"

"Because you didn't want to tell Mum. That's why."

Jo looked at his feet. "Mum doesn't have to know everything, Dan."

"But we can't go on a tour with Sam, Jo. He's only a kid like us!"

"He's got a driver's licence," Jo told his brother and looked at Sam.

"Yeah, that's right," Sam said. "You can get your licence when you're 15 in New Zealand. And I'm 16. Come on Dan. I know all the best places. It'll be all right."

"No, Mum won't like it. Come on, Jo. Let's get out and go over to Turoa's."

"No, I'm staying here," Jo said.

"I'll call Mum and tell her, Jo. Then you'll be in trouble."

Jo said nothing.

Dan opened the door and got out of the car. When he closed the door, the car drove off.

Chapter 11 The river

Jo, Sam and Jessie were all very quiet as they drove out of Queenstown. The sun disappeared behind some clouds and the morning was suddenly dark and grey. Then, after a few minutes, Sam said, "Your brother is a bit of a mummy's boy, eh?"

"Stop it, Sam," said Jessie. "Maybe we should go back. You know you can't …"

"Oh, come on, Jessie," Sam said. "I can't what? I know what I'm doing. Jo? What do you think?"

Jo looked out of the window. He felt a bit sad now, but he didn't want go back and see his brother's face. Not after that argument. "No, let's do it," he said. "We don't have to do a really long tour, right?"

"Right," Sam agreed. "We can be back for lunch."

And Sam really did know some good Lord of the Rings locations. They went to the scene of one of the big battles and to the place where Saruman's tower, Isengard, stood in the film. Sam drove carefully and Jo soon forgot all about his argument with Dan.

At about twelve o'clock, they were on a dirt road next to a small river. Sam drove slowly. "We go across the river near here," he said, "and then up into that forest over there. That's the forest of Lothlorien in the film."

"Right," said Jo. He could see the road on the other side of the river.

Sam turned the car and started to drive slowly across the river. In the middle, the car stopped. Sam looked worried and put his hand over his mouth.

Jo laughed. "I know that trick," he said. "Mike did it on the tour last week too."

But this time it wasn't a trick. Sam tried to drive across the river. The motor was really loud, the wheels spun round and round, but the car didn't move.

Sam looked at Jessie and Jo. "We're stuck," he told them.

"Stuck?" Jessie said. She looked really scared. "What can we do?"

"OK, you two get out and try to push," Sam said. "There must be a big rock in the river. If you push, perhaps we can get over it."

"How can we push in the middle of a river?" Jo asked.

"It's not deep," Sam said.

He was right. The water was only 20 or 30 centimetres deep. So Jessie and Jo got out and stood behind the car and started to push. It didn't help and five minutes later they got back in again. Their feet were wet and very cold.

"That water is freezing," Jo said.

"Yeah, and it's colder outside now too," Jessie said. "What do we do now?"

"Well," said Sam, "I suppose we'll have to walk back to the main road and get help."

Jessie shook her head. "It's 10 kilometres back to the road, Sam. It'll take hours. Let's stay here and wait."

"We can't do that," Sam told her. "What if nobody comes along here today? We can't stay here all night. What do you think, Jo?"

"I don't know," he said and shook his head too. "My shoes are wet. My feet are cold. I don't really want to walk ten kilometres."

The three children sat in the car. Nobody said a word as snow started to fall from the grey sky.

After the others left him in the street in front of the shoe shop, Dan just stood there for a few minutes. Then he thought, "I must call Mum," and put his hand into his pocket – but there was nothing there. Jo had their mobile!

So he decided to walk to Turoa's and tell Turoa and Eileen. When he got there half an hour later, he was cold. It was windy and a lot of clouds covered the sky.

He knocked on the door and Eileen shouted from inside. "It's open."

Dan went in and Eileen gave him a big smile. "Er … Jo?"

"No, I'm Dan."

"Dan. Nice to see you. Is Jo with you?"

"No. No, he isn't. That's why I'm here."

Eileen saw how serious Dan looked. "Come and sit down here, Dan," she said. "Now, what's wrong, dear?"

Dan told her about Jo and Sam and Jessie and their Lord of the Rings tour. Eileen shook her head. "Just a minute," she said and got up and went outside. When she came back in, she said, "You're right. Sam's taken the car. What a stupid thing to do!"

"But he's got a driver's licence, right?" Dan said. "That's what he said."

"Oh, yes," Eileen answered. "He's got his licence – but it's not a full licence. So he's not allowed to carry passengers in the car, not alone. Someone with a full licence has to be in the car with him. He can't drive a couple of other kids around. Right, let's call Turoa. And your mum."

Eileen called her husband and told him the story.

"He's at work, but he's coming home right now," she said. "Now, let's try your mum."

But they couldn't reach Mrs Thompson on her mobile phone.

"This is New Zealand, dear," Eileen explained. "Your mum's off on a tour out in the country. Mobile phones don't work out there. You have to be in town."

Dan looked very worried. "But what can we do, then?"

"Don't worry, dear. I'll call her office. They can get her on the radio."

Snow covered the car in the middle of the small river.

"I'm cold," Jessie said. "Can't you turn the heater on?"

"OK," Sam said and started the car. A few minutes later it was nice and warm.

"How long will it be before they start to look for us?" Jo asked.

"They won't know where to look," Jessie said. She sounded very scared. "People die out here in the bush, you know."

"We won't die," Sam told her, but he didn't sound very sure about it.

"Maybe Dan phoned my mum and told her," Jo went on. "I'm sure they'll find us soon."

Then he felt something in his pocket. He took it out and held it up with a big smile on his face.

"Look what I've got!" he said.

Jessie and Sam looked at his mobile and both shook their heads. Jessie took her mobile out of her bag.

"No signal," she said and showed it to Jo. "Mobiles don't work out here in the bush."

Jo looked at his phone. She was right – there was no signal.

When she got the news over the radio, Mrs Thompson went back to the office in Queenstown at once. Ten minutes later, she was at Turoa's house. Pita was with her.

"When did they leave, Dan?" Mrs Thompson asked.

"About ten o'clock, Mum."

She looked at her watch. "OK, it's twelve now. Did they say where they wanted to go?"

"Their own Lord of the Rings tour," Dan said. "That's what Sam called it."

"He knows all your tours, Cathy," Turoa said. "They could be anywhere."

"We only have three different ones, Turoa," Mrs Thompson said. "What do you think, Pita? What do we do?"

Pita looked out the window. "The snow's getting worse," he said. "Mike will help. We can take three cars and search the tour routes for them. But …"

"But?" Mrs Thompson asked.

"Well, if we don't find them by one thirty, we'll have to call the search and rescue service. Get a helicopter. Before it gets too dark. Or the snow gets too bad."

"Right," Mrs Thompson said. "Let's go. Turoa, will you come with me?"

"Yes, OK."

"Me too Mum," said Dan.

"No, love, sorry. You stay here with Eileen."

"Oh, Mum! He's my brother, you know."

"I know, Dan. But I want to know that you're safe here with Eileen. All right? One son out in the bush is enough for one day."

"And don't worry, Dan," Pita said. "They're probably on their way back right now."

The car in the river was white with snow. Sam opened the door and looked down at the water.

"What are you doing?" Jessie asked. "It's cold, remember?"

"Yeah, I know. But rivers can get higher, right? I'm just checking, that's all."

"And?" Jessie said. "Is it getting higher?"

"Oh, only a little bit. A centimetre or so, I think. Maybe we should walk back to the road," Sam said.

"Don't be silly, Sam," Jessie said. "In this weather? We haven't got the right clothes, or shoes. It's too cold. And the river will only get higher if it rains."

"I could go alone," Sam went on. "I could jog back to the road in an hour."

"No, Sam. Jessie's right," Jo said. "We must stay together. And stay in the car. It's safer. It's easier to see the car, you know, when they start to look for us."

"Maybe," Sam said. "But the car is covered in snow. It won't be easy to see it."

"Well," Jo said, "it's twelve thirty now. Let's wait for another hour and then decide. Perhaps the snow will stop."

They waited quietly for half an hour. Then Sam put a CD in the CD player. "How about some music?" he said.

No one answered, so Sam turned up the volume, closed his eyes and tried to forget about everything except the song.

The music was so loud that they didn't hear the car on the road next to the river.

Suddenly the driver's door opened and Pita put his head in. "What, having a party?" he said. He smiled, but only for a second. "Right, all of you – get out and walk back across the river and get in my car. Now."

When they were all in his car, Pita went back to the other car in the middle of the river. Sam shouted to him out the window. "It's stuck, Pita. It won't move."

Pita just got in and started the car. He tried to move forwards, but the wheels just spun round and the car didn't move. So he tried to move backwards. Then forwards again, Slowly the car moved a little, backwards and forwards, backwards and forwards. And then, suddenly, it moved backwards across the river. Pita drove backwards on to the dirt road and parked the car. Then he walked over to the other car and got in.

"You're all in trouble," he said. "Big trouble."

"Shall I drive Grandad's car back?" Sam asked.

"No way," Pita answered. "You haven't got a licence any more, boy. You aren't allowed to take passengers with you, you know that. So you haven't got a licence any more. Right? We'll get Turoa's car later."

Chapter 12 The West Coast

Mrs Thompson was very angry with Jo when he came back home with Pita. She shouted at him.

"How could you be so stupid, Jo? I told you before: you can't just go off alone like that in New Zealand. The countryside here is not like England. It's empty. There's no one there. It's dangerous. If you get lost you can die. People die in the bush here every year, Jo."

Jo just looked at his feet. Then Mrs Thompson suddenly started to cry and went over to Jo and gave him a big hug. "I was so scared, Jo. I was so scared."

"I'm sorry, Mum. I'm sorry."

Three days later, they packed the car for their trip. They drove through the beautiful countryside past a few small towns and two huge lakes. It started to rain quite hard and they couldn't see the other side of the lakes. They drove on and in the late afternoon stopped for the night.

They were up early the next morning. There was more snow on the mountains now and it was very cold. They drove up into the mountains towards Haast Pass. Soon there was some snow on the road and then more and more. The snow was wet and heavy on the trees. Suddenly Mrs Thompson saw three or four cars on the road in front of them. They were stopped. In front of the first car, a tree lay across the road.

"Oh, no," said Mrs Thompson.

"Will we have to go back, Mum?" Dan asked.

"Yes, I think so. They'll probably close the road with all this snow."

Mrs Thompson and the kids got out of the car and walked over to the group of people next to the tree.

"G'day," said a man in a hat and black and red shirt. "As you can see, we can't get past this tree, but we think we can do something about that. Jason's got a chainsaw."

Another man came back from his small truck with a big chainsaw.

"OK," he said, "let's get this tree out of the way."

For the next half an hour the two men worked on the tree with the chainsaw. A couple of others pushed the pieces of tree off the side of the road and into the forest. Soon the road was clear again, and the cars moved slowly on to Haast Pass and down towards Haast Village. They went past a big sign. It said "ROAD CLOSED". When they arrived in Haast Village, there was no more snow on the road and it was much warmer.

Mrs Thompson drove for another couple of hours up the West Coast. There were almost no cars on the road on this grey day. They passed one about every ten minutes, but when they reached the small town of Fox Glacier, things looked busier. Twenty minutes later they were in another small town, Franz Josef, and it was full of tourists and tourist buses.

"Tourists love the glaciers," Mrs Thompson said. "It's always busy here. Let's have something to eat in town. Then we won't have to cook tonight."

She stopped the car and they all got out and had a walk around the little town. They went into a nice warm restaurant and had dinner. When they came out, it was raining again. They got in the car and drove on to Okarito.

Okarito was a very small village of about twenty houses. One of them was called Scottie's Cottage and that was where Mrs Thompson stopped the car. Behind the cottage was a big, flat piece of grass, hundreds of metres long, and behind that was the sea.

Dan and Jo ran across the grass to the water. There was a long beach, full of old wood and trees. The waves were huge and looked really dangerous.

They went back to help their mum. They unpacked the car and took everything inside. It was cold in there, but their mum soon had a fire in the big oven and half an hour later the cottage was nice and warm.

Mrs Thompson made some hot chocolate and they sat at the table in the kitchen and talked about their trip.

"We'll go to Franz Josef glacier tomorrow," the twins' mum said. "We'll walk through the forest first, up to the end of the glacier. It's so lovely. Then we'll do a half-day glacier walk. You'll love it."

The hot chocolate made the boys sleepy and they soon went to bed.

A really loud noise woke Dan and Jo the next morning.

"What is it?" Jo asked.

"I don't know," said Dan. "Another earthquake?"

The noise got louder and louder. They both got up and looked out the window. They could see a small red plane.

"It's crashing!" Jo shouted.

They both moved back from the window. The red plane landed on the grass behind the cottage and then turned round and stopped next to a house, about 30 metres away.

Dan and Jo went into the kitchen. Their mum was at the table with some tea and her book.

"Mum," shouted Jo. "Didn't you hear it? A plane just landed behind the cottage."

"Yes, I heard it," Mrs Thompson said and laughed. "That's the neighbour. He lives in Christchurch. He always comes here to his holiday home by plane."

After breakfast they drove back to Franz Josef and started their walk into the rain forest. It was a nice day with just a few clouds. In the forest everything looked green, even the sun. They went across lots of little bridges over streams and rivers. The tree trunks were all green. Things grew everywhere and everything was wet.

For forty-five minutes they walked through the forest, then they came out into a big valley and saw the mountains in the sun.

"There's Mount Cook," Mrs Thompson said.

"Aoraki, we call it," Jo said, and laughed.

They walked along the glacier valley. Waterfalls crashed down from the grey mountains on both sides of the valley. A big river ran through the centre. Its water was white, almost like milk.

"That river comes out at the end of the glacier," Mrs Thompson told the twins. "We'll see the glacier soon."

They walked on up the valley, and went round a bend and there was Franz Josef glacier. The end of it looked dirty grey but higher up it shone white in the sun.

"Do we have to do a tour, Mum?" Jo asked. "Can't we just walk on to the glacier on our own?"

"No, we can't," Mrs Thompson said. "Glaciers can be very dangerous. They're full of holes and crevasses. You can fall down a hole and end up in the river. And when we're on the tour, Jo, you do what the tour guides say. OK?"

"OK, Mum."

An hour later, Mrs Thompson, Dan and Jo were standing on Franz Josef glacier in their special glacier boots. It was a warm day in the forest and the glacier valley, but when they walked out on to the glacier, a very cold wind came down from the mountains.

"It's freezing," said Jo.

"Oh, you'll be warm soon, mate," said the tour guide. "When we go up, up there." He pointed up the glacier.

With the other tourists, they followed the guide. He made a track on the ice for them and told them all about the glacier every time they stopped.

After a while, they were much warmer again.

They saw holes and crevasses and even walked through a few crevasses.

"This is fantastic," said Jo. "Mum, let's take some photos."

They took thirty or forty photos on Jo's digital camera.

By the time they got down off the glacier again, they were all very tired, but they still had to walk back through the rain forest to Franz Josef village. When they arrived, it was almost dark. They went into a café for a cup of tea.

Dan bought a postcard and they all wrote something to the twins' dad.

Hi Dad, Franz Josef was the best part of our trip. We walked through a couple of crevasses. One was so small, we had to walk sideways. I can't wait to show you the photos! Jo

Hi Dad, How are you? We're having a great time on the West Coast with Mum. We're staying in a lovely little cottage in Okarito. The neighbour arrived by plane this morning. Love, Dan

Dear Michael, I'm so glad Dan and Jo could come. We're having a wonderful time together. They like NZ, I think, but they miss Bristol and you too. Cathy

Chapter 13 End of the trip

When they left Franz Josef and Okarito they drove slowly back to Queenstown. It took two days and Dan and Jo only had a few days left in New Zealand now.

The next day the twins went into town. They wanted to buy some presents for their dad and their friends back in Bristol. It took them a long time, but in the end they found a nice present for everyone.

"What did you get?" Mrs Thompson asked them when she came home that afternoon.

"Jack is a big Lord of the Rings fan," Jo said. "So we got him that book about all the film locations."

"Yes, Mum, it's a great book," Dan said. "They've got photos in it of all the places on your tour."

"That's a nice present. What did you get the girls?"

"Well, Ananda loves honey," Dan said. "So we bought her some of that special New Zealand honey."

"Oh, manuka honey. It's really good for you."

"And we got this paua shell for Sophie," Jo said.

"Lovely! And for your dad?"

"This New Zealand calendar. It's got amazing photos in it. And we've seen some of the places," Dan said.

"Yeah, and we'll tell him we have to come back and see the others another time," said Jo.

"Yes," said Mrs Thompson and put her arms round her two sons, "yes, you tell him that."

"Mum?" said Dan.

"Yes, dear?"

"Do you miss Bristol sometimes?"

"Of course I do, love," Mrs Thompson answered. "But I love it here in New Zealand too. And you know, your dad and I just weren't very happy together in Bristol. Not in the end."

"Yes, I know," Dan said. He looked very sad.

Jo asked, "Are you happy here, Mum?"

Mrs Thompson thought for a minute. "Yes, I am. I'm happy here. I like my job and I like Queenstown. It's so lovely, and ..."

Dan looked at her. "What about Pita?" he asked.

"Yes, I like Pita, Dan," she said.

"I like him too," Jo said. "He's really nice."

Dan looked at his mum. "Yes, he is nice. But I miss you, Mum."

Mrs Thompson took Dan's hands. "I know, Dan. I know. But you know, you can always come here, to Queenstown, if you want."

"What, come and live here and go to school with Jessie and Sam?" Dan asked.

"Why not? It's a good school," Mrs Thompson said.

"Really?" Jo said. "Could we?"

"Yes. If you want to, I can talk to your dad."

"Cool," said Jo.

Dan wasn't so sure. "I don't know. We're not from here. They talk, you know, different. And it's not really home."

"But maybe you could try it for six months, Dan," his mum said. "You know, just give it a try."

"All right. Maybe, Mum. I can think about it."

Two days later, Pita and Mrs Thompson drove the twins back to Christchurch Airport and it was time to say goodbye.

"OK, I'll leave you three alone now and go back to the car," Pita said. He gave Dan and Jo a big hug. "See you next time, guys, eh?"

Dan and Jo and Mrs Thompson didn't say anything for a while. They all had tears in their eyes.

"All right, boys," said Mrs Thompson at last. "It's time to go. Be good boys. Take care. Say hello to everyone in Bristol from me. And, you think about it, eh, Dan? Remember, you can come to Queenstown if you want. No worries, eh?"

"No worries," said Jo.

"We'll think about it, Mum," said Dan.

And they walked away to get their plane.

When Mr Shaw picked them up at London Airport more than 24 hours later, Dan was soon asleep in the car.

"Aren't you tired too, Jo?" their dad asked.

"No, I slept on the plane, Dad. Dan was up all night. Lord of the Rings."

"What?" Mr Shaw said, "He watched Lord of the Rings films all night? Like you did on the way to New Zealand?"

"No, Dad," said Jo. "He read the book."

Vocabulary

A

across [ə'krɒs] quer, über
age [eɪdʒ] Alter
(to) **be allowed to do sth.** [ə'laʊd] etwas tun dürfen
airport ['eəpɔːt] Flughafen
along [ə'lɒŋ] entlang
argument ['ɑːgjʊmənt] Streit, Auseinandersetzung
(to) **arrive** [ə'raɪv] ankommen
at once [ət 'wʌns] sofort
awake [ə'weɪk] wach
axe [æks] Axt

B

backwards ['bækwədz] nach hinten, rückwärts
(to) **begin** [bɪ'gɪn] anfangen, beginnen
began [bɪ'gæn] Vergangenheitsform von „begin"
(to) **borrow** ['bɒrəʊ] (sich) borgen, (sich) ausleihen
bungy jumping ['bʌndʒi dʒʌmpɪŋ] Bungee-Springen
bush: the bush [bʊʃ] Busch, Urwald (*z. B. Gebiet an der Westküste der Südinsel Neuseelands*)
busy ['bɪzi] *hier:* hektisch

C

cabbage tree ['kæbɪdʒ triː] Kohlbaum (*eine palmenähnliche Pflanze*)
central heating [ˌsentrəl 'hiːtɪŋ] Zentralheizung
chainsaw ['tʃeɪnsɔː] Kettensäge
chook [tʃʊk] (*Neuseeland*) Hähnchen
(to) **chop** [tʃɒp] hacken
coast [kəʊst] Küste
coffee ['kɒfi] Kaffee
cottage ['kɒtɪdʒ] Häuschen, Cottage
a couple of ['kʌpl] ein paar
(to) **cover** ['kʌvə] bedecken, abdecken
(to) **crash** [kræʃ] *hier:* abstürzen
crevasse [krə'væs] Gletscherspalte
cup [kʌp] Tasse
curtain ['kɜːtn] Vorhang
customs ['kʌstəmz] Zoll
customs officer ['kʌstəmz‿ˌɒfɪsə] Zollbeamter/in

D

deep [diːp] tief
delicious [dɪ'lɪʃəs] köstlich, lecker
(to) **dig** [dɪg] graben
dirt road ['dɜːt rəʊd] unbefestigte Straße

driver's licence ['draɪvəz laɪsənz] Führerschein
dwarf [dwɔːf] Zwerg

E

earth [ɜːθ] Erde
earthquake ['ɜːθkweɪk] Erdbeben
edge [edʒ] Rand, Kante; *hier:* Ufer
elven ['elvən] elfenhaft

F

fern [fɜːn] Farn
flat white ['flæt waɪt] (*Australien/ Neuseeland*) Milchkaffee
flood [flʌd] Flut
foil [fɔɪl] Alufolie
folks *(pl)* [fəʊks] (*infml*) Leute
forecast ['fɔːkɑːst] (Wetter-)Vorhersage
(to) **forget** [fə'get] vergessen
forwards ['fɔːwədz] vorwärts
freezing ['friːzɪŋ] eiskalt

G

G'day [gə'deɪ] (*Neuseeland*) hallo
(to) **get lost** [lɒst] sich verirren
(to) **get out (of)** *hier:* aussteigen
(to) **give sb. a hug** [hʌg] jn. umarmen
glacier ['glæsiə] Gletscher
(to) **go off** (los)gehen, (los)fahren
(to) **grab** [græb] greifen (nach)
grass [grɑːs] Gras
(to) **grow** [grəʊ] *hier:* werden
guide [gaɪd] Reiseleiter/in, Fremdenführer/in
guys *(pl)* [gaɪz] (*infml, als Anrede*) Leute

H

half: (to) **cut in half** [hɑːf] halbieren
hangi ['hʌŋi] *traditionelles Maori Festessen, auf heißen Steinen unter der Erde gegart*
(to) **hang out** [hæŋ] (*infml*) rumhängen, sich rumtreiben
headphones ['hedfəʊnz] Kopfhörer
heater [hiːtə] Heizung, Heizkörper
heavy ['hevi] schwer
high [haɪ] hoch
honey; manuka honey ['hʌni; 'mʌnʊːkʌ ˌhʌni] Honig; Manuka-Honig (*aus den Blüten des Teebaums gewonnen*)
hug [hʌg] Umarmung
huge [hjuːdʒ] riesig

I

(to) **imagine sth.** [ɪ'mædʒɪn] sich etwas vorstellen
immigration officer [ˌɪmɪ'greɪ ʃn‿ˌɒfɪsə] Beamte/r der Einwanderungsbehörde

J

journey ['dʒɜːni] Reise

K

kia ora [ˌkɪə 'ɔ:rə] (*Maori, zu einer Person*) hallo, guten Tag

~ koutou [~ kəʊtəʊ] (*Maori, zu mehreren Leuten*) hallo, guten Tag

(to) **kiss** [kɪs] küssen

Kiwi ['ki:wi:] *hier:* Neuseeländer/in

kumara ['ku:mrʌ] (*Neuseeland*) Süßkartoffel

L

(to) **be left** [left] übrig sein

(to) **lie** [laɪ] liegen

lay [leɪ] Vergangenheitsform von „lie"

location [ləʊ'keɪʃn] *hier:* Drehort

long black schwarzer Kaffee

(to) **look like** aussehen wie

The Lord of the Rings [lɔ:d] „Der Herr der Ringe" (*Roman-Trilogie von J. R. R. Tolkien*)

love (*als Anrede*) Schatz

M

main (road) [meɪn] Hauptstraße

Maori ['maʊri] Maori (*Ureinwohner/innen Neuseelands*)

mate [meɪt] Kumpel

meal [mi:l] Mahlzeit

metal ['metl] Metall

microwave ['maɪkrəweɪv] Mikrowelle(nherd)

middle ['mɪdl] Mitte

motor ['məʊtə] Motor

O

old-fashioned [ˌəʊld'fæʃnd] altmodisch

office ['ɒfɪs] Büro

Orc [ɔ:k] Ork (*feindseliges Wesen in Tolkiens „Der Herr der Ringe"*)

P

Pakeha (*Maori*) weiße Menschen

palm (tree) [pɑ:m] Palme

Pasifika (*Maori*) Menschen von den Pazifischen Inseln

passenger ['pæsɪndʒə] *hier:* Mitfahrer

paua (shell) ['pɑ:ʊa] Paua-Muschel

(to) **pierce** [pɪəs] durchstechen

piercer: cloud piercer „Wolkendurchstecher" (*engl. Übersetzung des Maori Namens für den Mount Cook (Maori: Aoraki)*)

pillow ['pɪləʊ] Kopfkissen

platform ['plætfɔ:m] Plattform (*hier: für den Absprung beim Bungee-Springen*)

Pom (Pommy) [pɒm] (*infml, Australien/Neuseeland*) Engländer/in

R

(to) **reach** [ri:tʃ] erreichen, ankommen

(to) **realize** ['ri:əlaɪz] erkennen, wahrnehmen

roof [ru:f] Dach

rope [rəʊp] Seil

S

school report Schulzeugnis
(to) **scream** [skri:m] schreien
search and rescue service [ˌsɜ:tʃ‿ənd 'reskju: ˌsɜ:vɪs] Rettungsdienst
seat [si:t] Sitzplatz
serious ['sɪəriəs] ernsthaft
(to) **shake hands with sb.** [ʃeɪk] jm. die Hand geben/schütteln
should [ʃʊd] soll(en), sollte(n)
sideways ['saɪdweɪz] seitwärts
south [saʊθ] Süden, südlich
special ['speʃl] speziell, besonders
(to) **spin** [spɪn] sich drehen
spun [spʌn] Vergangenheitsform von „spin"
square [skweə] Quadrat-, quadratisch
steam [sti:m] Dampf
stone [stəʊn] Stein
strange [streɪndʒ] seltsam; fremd
stream [stri:m] Bach
(to) **be stuck** [stʌk] feststecken, -sitzen
stupid ['stju:pɪd] dumm, blöd
(to) **suggest** [sə'dʒest] vorschlagen
(to) **suppose** [sə'pəʊz] vermuten; *hier:* glauben, meinen

T

(to) **take** *hier:* dauern, (*Zeit*) in Anspruch nehmen
takeaway ['teɪkəweɪ] *hier:* Essen zum Mitnehmen
tear [tɪə] Träne
thick [θɪk] dick
(to) **tie** [taɪ] binden, befestigen
(to) **touch** [tʌtʃ] berühren, anfassen
towel ['taʊəl] Handtuch
track [træk] Spur, Weg
traditional [trə'dɪʃənl] traditionell
(tree) trunk [trʌŋk] (Baum-) Stamm

U

(to) **unpack** [ˌʌn'pæk] auspacken

V

vegetable ['vedʒtəbl] Gemüse

W

walking shoes Wanderschuhe
(to) **wake sb. (up)** [weɪk] jn. (auf)wecken
(to) **wake up** aufwachen
waterfall ['wɔ:təfɔ:l] Wasserfall
wave [weɪv] Welle
way [weɪ] Weg
way: on the way auf dem Weg
(to) **weigh** [weɪ] wiegen
west [west] Westen, westlich
wet [wet] nass
(to) **wink** [wɪŋk] zwinkern
(to) **be worried** besorgt sein, sich Sorgen machen
no worries kein Problem, keine Ursache

Names

Aoraki [ʌɔː'rʌki]
Aotearoa ['ʌɔːterʌˌrɔːʌ]
Arrow River ['ærəʊ rɪvə]
Billy ['bɪli]
Christchurch ['kraɪsttʃɜːtʃ]
Eileen ['aɪliːn, aɪ'liːn]
Franz Josef [frænts 'dʒəʊzɪf]
Geraldine ['dʒerəldiːn]
Haast Pass ['hɑːst pɑːs]
Jessie ['dʒesi]
Kawarau Bridge ['kʌwərɔː ˌbridʒ]
Lake Wakatipu [ˌleɪk wɒkʌ'tipʊ]
Mike [maɪk]
Mount Cook [ˌmaʊnt 'kʊk]
Okarito [ɒkʌ'riːtɒ]
Pita ['piːtə]
Queenstown ['kwiːnztaʊn]
Sam [sæm]
Scottie ['skɒti]
Singapore [ˌsɪŋə'pɔː]
Turoa [tʊ'rɔːʌ]

Check your understanding

Chapter 1:

1) Describe Dan's dream.
2) What does Jo do on the plane? And Dan?
3) Compare what the two boys think when they look out the window.

Chapter 2:

1) What does Jo tell the first immigration officer?
2) Why is Jo happy when they go through customs?
3) How do you know how Mrs Thompson feels when she sees the twins?

Chapter 3:

1) Why do Mrs Thompson, Pita and Dan all laugh about Jo?
2) Find three New Zealand words (Maori or English) and explain what they mean.
3) Why do you think Jo is gone?

Chapter 4:

1) Who finds Jo and where?
2) What does Dan's dream mean?
3) Describe what the two boys realize because of the weather.

Chapter 5:

1) How do the twins have fun after they wake up?
2) Who wants to do what? What does this tell you about them?

Chapter 6:

1) Describe the steps of a hangi.
2) Name some New Zealand food words.
3) Who are Sam and Jessie? What do you find out about them?

Chapter 7:

1) Compare Jo and Dan's opinion of the Lord of the Rings books and films. Who do you agree with?
2) In two or three sentences, describe a Lord of the Rings tour.
3) What trick does Mike play on Jo?

Chapter 8:

1) What facts do you find out about bungy jumping?
2) This chapter shows us that Dan and Jo are quite different. How are they different?

Chapter 9:

1) Write Jo and Granny's chat in correct English.
2) When can you get a driver's licence in Germany?
3) Should Jo and Dan go with Sam and Jessie? Why? Why not?

Chapter 10:

1) Have you ever felt an earthquake? What happened?
2) Why does Jo want to go into town and not to Turoa's house?
3) Choose Sam or Jessie. What are they thinking when Jo and Dan are arguing?

Chapter 11

1) Write a timeline for Jo and Dan's day.
2) Should the kids leave the car in the river and walk to the main road? What are the arguments for and against?
3) Explain why they cannot phone for help.
4) How do you know what Pita feels when he finds them?

Chapter 12

1) Describe what happens on the way to the West Coast.
2) How does the neighbour in Okarito arrive?
3) Imagine Dan has to write a story about this day for school. Make notes for his story.

Chapter 13

1) What will the Bristol kids think of their presents?
2) Do you think Dan and Jo will come to live in New Zealand? Why? Why not?

Questions on the whole story

1) Find two facts about New Zealand which:
   – surprised you.
   – you think are cool.
   – you think are silly.
2) Choose a person (Dan, Jo, or Mrs Thompson) and describe how they change in the story.
3) Which place in New Zealand would you most like to visit? Explain why.
4) Choose three adjectives that best describe the story for you.
5) Imagine you are Jo. Write a letter about your Lord of the Rings tour with Sam and Jessie.
6) Choose the funniest/most exciting/most boring/... scene in the story. Describe it to a partner and explain why you think it is funny/exciting/...